The Wisdom

of

Ramana Maharshi

A Modern Sufi Rendition

by

Shaykh Fadhlalla Haeri

Zahra Publications

Distributed & Published by Zahra Publications
Centurion
South Africa

E-mail: zp@sfhfoundation.com
info@zahrapublications.pub
© 2021 Shaykh Fadhlalla Haeri

Designed and typeset in South Africa by
Mizpah Marketing Concepts

To purchase an eBook or printed version of this book,
please visit www.zahrapublications.pub

For further information on Shaykh Fadhlalla Haeri and
his teaching please visit www.sfhfoundation.com

ISBN: 978-1-928329-33-6

Table of Contents

The Wisdom of Ramana Maharshi

Introduction

As a young student in the late 1950s in Britain, I came across a slim volume of teachings from Bhagvan Ramana Maharshi which impressed me greatly. This was the booklet 'Truth Revealed – Sad-Vidya'. Years later I was sent a new edition of the book with a picture of Ramana Maharshi on it which gave me much joy. After all these years, after I had begun to discover the truth of his teachings, I thought it would be useful to refresh some of the language, which was cast in traditional Hindu idiom, into a contemporary vernacular that could be of use in a wider context. This effort is what is now in your hands.

The journey of human beings on earth is part of the process that links us to the infinite unseen through our own soul or spirit within the limitations of the material world, governed by our mind so as to enable us to function on earth. The human journey is to accept these limitations but equally and more importantly to open up to the intuitions and lights that inspire us and give us a touch of the timeless, boundless nature of our own souls.

This book makes accessible to most people a universal exposure to the highest consciousness. We are in a sense climbing a ladder of light towards a pure and cosmic origin. This ladder is composed of strands of intelligence based on sincerity, honesty and courage. Depending on how one ascends each one of us will arrive at a stage which is truly deserved before returning to higher consciousness through the generous gateway of death.

During the past few thousand years human consciousness has been rising in awareness and intelligence to points that almost transcend the simple inquiry as to who we are and what is the end of our life. In many cultures individuals or prophets have taken this rise of consciousness to a point where there is hardly any other option other than to accept the rational the basic human consciousness, with all its limitations, and at the same time to try to transcend it to a level beyond cause and effect, where the original light of pure consciousness shines upon all.

Ramana Maharshi is one of the pure beings who had done this fairly recently, having emerged from a Hindu culture but influenced people all over the world. It is hoped that this booklet makes his insights more accessible to present day English speakers while maintaining the original meaning and purpose of his utterances.

Shaykh Fadhlalla Haeri,
September 2021

Sri Ramana Maharshi

Bhagavan Sri Ramana Maharshi was born on 30 December 1879 as Venkataraman Iyer in Tiruchuli, Tamil Nadu. He was an Indian Hindu sage and jivanmukta (liberated being).

As a young man he developed an attraction to the sacred hill of Arunachala and the 63 sages of Siva or Nyanmars. In 1896, at the age of 16, he had a "death-experience" where he became aware of a "force" which he recognized as his true "I" or "self", and which he later identified with "the personal God, or Iswara". This resulted in a state that he later described as "the state of mind of Iswara". Six weeks later he left his uncle's home in Madurai, and journeyed to the holy mountain Arunachala, in Tiruvannamalai, where he took on the role of a religious mendicant for the rest of his life.

He attracted devotees that regarded him as an avatar and came to him for "the sight of God". In later years an ashram grew up around him, where visitors received spiritual instruction by sitting silently in his company asking questions. Since the 1930s his teachings have been popularized in the West, resulting in his worldwide recognition as an enlightened being.

Bhagavan Sri Ramana Maharshi approved a number of paths and practices, but recommended self-enquiry as the principal means to remove ignorance and abide in Self-awareness, together with devotion or surrender to the Self. Bhagavan Sri Ramana Maharshi died on 14 April 1950.

Part One

Synopsis

i. *Earthly reality is experienced through the mind. Higher cosmic Reality is transmitted through the soul and the heart.*

ii. *The nature of your soul is immortal and to know that you have to turn away completely from the egocentric and transient identity.*

~ 1 ~

There is no distance or separation between supreme Reality and all that is known and unknown.

~ 2 ~

The ego-self is the earthly side of a duality, whose heavenly origin is the divine soul within the heart, which can be awakened to by transcending the lower self and the illusion of separation.

~ 3 ~

If your aim is to awaken to the eternal Reality then you have to turn away from all manifestations and temporary appearances of that reality.

~ 4 ~

The essence of every form is pure energy and to realise that truth you need to perceive every material form has emerged from that original energy.

~ 5 ~

Your physical and mental state constantly relate to the outer world around you.

~ 6 ~

Your mind's capacity is directed toward the world that is experienced in order to understand and respond to it.

~ 7 ~

Knowledge of dualities is a prelude to perceiving the light of Oneness which illumines the entire universe.

~ 8 ~

Worshipping, praying and meditating upon higher meaning and consciousness is a prelude to realising cosmic Oneness.

~ 9 ~

Duality is consistently the source of confusion and challenge to discover the light of unity transmitted from the soul within the heart.

~ 10 ~

Knowledge enables us to discover earthly causalities, as well as a higher unitive reality and the source of all knowledges and existences.

~ 11 ~

The human self is a joint venture between the divine soul within the heart and its earthly shadow, which is the personal identity and evolving human in us.

~ 12 ~

The soul knows all but its shadow (the ego-self) is concerned only with earthly subsistence and survival.

~ 13 ~

Your real self or soul is a divine light that gives rise to the shadowy earthly self and its constant struggle with dualities and self-preservation.

~ 14 ~

Diversities and dualities are transient outer manifestations whose inner reality is the light of cosmic Oneness.

~ 15 ~

The present moment is eternally present within timelessness and thus contains all past and future situations.

~ 16 ~

Your lower-self relates to the transitory world, yet its source of life is boundless and timeless.

~ 17 ~

The so-called "I" refers to the human transit on earth, as well as the eternal life which has empowered it.

~ 18 ~

The outer transitory reality is what everyone considers to be normal and real. To the awakened being, however, reality is constant, eternal and absolute.

~ 19 ~

As part of the evolution toward supreme consciousness we seek freedom and hope for a good destiny, which is the absolute truth.

~ 20 ~

The soul and its light is so powerful that it can only be known through veils and barriers moderated by the mind and the illusion of separation and self-identity.

~ 21 ~

Personal identity and the illusion of independence from the heavenly essence causes much suffering, as well as the drive to transcend it to the light of the Source which is within you as a soul.

~ 22 ~

Light of the mind is modified divine light transmitted from the soul within the heart and to realise that truth you need to switch your mind off completely.

~ 23 ~

What you are seeking is the original divine light within you from which the ideas of body and mind had arisen.

~ 24 ~

The ego-self is a mere cover and a drive toward the divine and permanent soul.

~ 25 ~

Humanity and its changing identities are mere shadows of the permanent divine soul within your own heart.

~ 26/27 ~

The ultimate transcendence from the lower self to the higher soul is fueled by your constant inquiry as to the nature of the shadow self and its real source.

~ 28 ~

To transcend the self and experience your soul you need vigilance and constant focus on the ego shadow that will disappear by itself as the light of your soul ascends.

~ 29 ~

Through constant meditation, reflection and silence you will realise that the source of your existence is not separate from the cosmic source itself.

~ 30 ~

To transcend the ego-self we need to focus upon higher consciousness, starting with specific insights and openings.

~ 31 ~

Through clear mind and senses we attain earthly wisdom, through insight and purity at heart the light of the soul reveals the fickle nature of the ego-self and its transience.

~ 32 ~

Our natural human drive to achieve and excel continues until the light of the inner soul directs that drive toward the infinite cosmic light, after that there is only clarity at every level of witnessing due to calibration with the absolute.

~ 33 ~

Meditation is like a ladder that takes you from the lower level of consciousness to the highest cosmic level, where all the known and the unknown is ever-present within that reality - the supreme divine miracle.

~ 34 ~

The so-called self and ego is only the outer shell of the inner soul or spirit which is eternal and divine.

~ 35 ~

You start the enquiry through reason, rationality and intelligence until you reach the subtler zone of your inner sprit with its full and boundless consciousness.

~ 36 ~

All outer realities and experiences are mere shadows reflecting the original divine patterns of energies, which are the source of all material transitory manifestations.

~ 37 ~

Supreme Reality and Truth pervades everything and needs no proof from anyone but the human drive to be content may help seekers to awaken to the Cosmic One as the cause and destiny of all.

~ 38 ~

The supreme Truth is ever-effulgent. It is only the mind and human condition that gives us the illusion of progress towards spiritual enlightenment.

~ 39 ~

The human drive to be liberated from fears, sorrow and other illusions will drive us to be watchful and alert rather than imagine independence. God is the only Source of all powers and constant reference to that Source will liberate us from the illusion of being the doer.

~ 40 ~

Whatever we experience of duality, such as good and bad or freedom and bondage, is the nature of earthly experiences. All that is physical, mental or emotional has its complementary opposite whereas the only true unique Oneness is present within each heart as a soul, which is the source of life.

~ 41 ~

So long as the soul is within the body there can be no complete liberation except through long periods of silence, meditation and transcendence of conditioned consciousness or physical death.

The Wisdom of Ramana Maharshi

Part Two

Synopsis

Reality and truth are absolute and boundless. Human consciousness arises from it and connects the absolute with limited human consciousness. Human quest begins with curiosity about what is useful and helpful for survival but ends in a zone where the celestial and terrestrial realms are One Divine Light.

~ 1 ~

The human being does not exist in isolation. Relationships exert powerful influences, constructively as well as destructively. A seeker of spiritual awakening will benefit much by being with those who are either awakened or on the same path.

~ 2 ~

Learning through books or reflection are not as potent as being with an awakened being.

~ 3 ~

Liberation from the lower-self or ego is more effective through close association with an enlightened being.

~ 4 ~

Trust in an enlightened one and serving in the way of truth can help to erode the dark shadows of the lower-self.

~ 5 ~

The light that is transmitted from an enlightened being may ignite your higher consciousness.

~ 6 ~

The light of the Supreme Governor of the universe resides in your own heart.

~ 7 ~

Your soul or spirit is the source of your life's consciousness and knowledge.

~ 8 ~

The light of supreme Reality radiates from your own soul and constant reference to that is the path to awakening.

~ 9 ~

When self-awareness is illumined by the light of the soul, the dark shadows of the ego will vanish.

~ 10 ~

Consciousness of the soul contains all lower and higher levels of consciousness.

~ 11 ~

Through awakening to the soul you are born to full consciousness and enlightenment.

~ 12 ~

Enlightenment is impossible if awareness and concern for one's physical and mental identity dominate consciousness.

~ 13 ~

Transcending lower basic consciousness to higher levels is the purpose of human life, especially for the spiritual seeker.

~ 14 ~

Awakening to the cosmic light within your own heart is the real drive that propels you towards better life, happiness and completing your life's purpose.

~ 15 ~

The desire for independence implies leaving your earthly identity, which is always dependent, and realizing your spiritual reality, which is beyond dependence and independence.

~ 16 ~

The full light of your own soul can only be realized by turning away from all shadows that distract you and veil your inner light.

~ 17 ~

The light of the Supreme Governor of the cosmos is in your own heart and to realize that is your purpose.

~ 18 ~

The light of your own soul is beaming through your inner heart, which is balanced by the physical heart within the breast.

~ 19 ~

The inner heart is the home of your soul and can be tarnished as a result of impure intentions and actions, which reduce the brilliance of the light of your soul.

~ 20 ~

There are two zones of consciousness. One is earth bound and relates to the physical and material realities. The other is timeless and boundless and belongs to the zone of the absolute Truth.

~ 21 ~

Your heart (due to the soul within it) will accept that which is true and reject that which is not.

~ 22 ~

The physical organ of the heart performs the vital function of sustaining biological existence, whereas the inner heart is what connects us to the cosmic spirit through the soul.

~ 23 ~

The entire universe is represented in you as your own soul, which resides within the heart.

~ 24 ~

The less we are affected by the ever changing shadows of the lower-self the more we are poised to connect with the light of the spirit within.

~ 25 ~

Deep refection upon the shadowy reality of attachment and desire leads to a point where the higher light of truth guides and attracts unto itself.

~ 26/27 ~

Our earthly life is transitory and is based on ever-changing shadows that connect matter and energy, interpreted by the mind which is energized by the soul.

~ 28 ~

The higher stage of enlightenment is knowledge that encompasses the timeless absolute, as well as the relative and transitory domains.

~ 29 ~

Those who are awakened to true knowledge are effective in action as well as in inaction; those who are not are encumbered within different levels of darkness or veils of the ego-self.

~ 30 ~

The enlightened being can only act through calibration and connectedness to the absolute Source of existence.

~ 31 ~

The enlightened person's thoughts and actions when guided by the soul transcend all the relative stages of consciousness and awakening.

~ 32 ~

The enlightened person's action is void of concern or reaction, as it is conducted in the pure flow of consciousness.

~ 33 ~

For him who transcended all dualities and discernments no worldly experience is of any consequence.

~ 34 ~

Earthly knowledge and education is limited
and useful only within the terrestrial domain.
Consequently it can be a major obstacle in
the process of awakening to boundless light
and knowledge.

~ 35 ~

Our worldly existence is balanced between
action and reaction but our spiritual Realty
transcends all that is within time and space.

~ 36 ~

Formal education and skills can often be an obstacle with regards to primal and absolute knowledge, as it strengthens one's identity and dependence on this knowledge.

~ 37 ~

The lower-self and ego is consistently treacherous and draws its nourishment from being admired and respected.

~ 38 ~

The enlightened being transcends the attraction of praise and repulsion of censure and criticism.

~ 39 ~

Understanding certain aspects of higher Reality may or may not help to awaken to it.

~ 40 ~

The ultimate wisdom is to recognize the tricky nature of the ego-self and to completely transcend it.

Part Three

Synopsis

Cosmic reality radiates numerous attributes, which hold the entire universe together and amongst those are life, knowledge and will. The human being carries the energy of the original evolutionary drive, which began in a single cell mutating and evolving into numerous plants, animals and leading to the human composition. Besides the physical heart within us there is a metaphorical heart, which is the home of the soul or spirit. This needs to be kept pure for the light of the soul to shine and lead, otherwise the darkness of lower self and ego will mislead. Fear and concern about death can lead to confusion and depression due to the exclusive identification with body and mind. Liberation comes with the discovery that in Reality you are an eternal soul.

~ 1 ~

In truth there is only the Absolute. God alone exists and no other. Every manifestation, form or energy emanates from It and due to Its will and power.

~ 2 ~

The Absolute is boundless and not subject to any limitations of space or time whereas our human experiences are conditioned within these constraints. From the Absolute, the soul or spirit emerges and causes the conditioned human experience of change and earthly temporary realities.

~ 3 ~

Our worldly realities are hazy versions of the Real. Our worldly consciousness is limited and conditioned, whereas durable joy lies only within the soul's zone of boundlessness. All human challenges occur within the limitations of space and time, whereas awakening to the truth and perpetual joy occurs when limited consciousness leads to full awakening.

~ 4 ~

In truth there is only the absolute boundlessness. For any notion of that to take place you need a diluted version of that light to reflect through the human soul and give rise to the ego; all in order to catch a glimpse of the cosmic Truth.

~ 5~

The amazing human body with its complex system of organs and their interactive connectedness is the instrument that will enable the soul via the modification of the mind, to bring about personal experiences and the rise of the ego-self, which is only a dim shadow of the soul.

~ 6 ~

Human experiences occur due to the interconnection between matter and energy via consciousness, which stretches from full consciousness to the simple sensory awareness.

~ 7 ~

Reality is absolute and has a cosmic network which we are also caught in through our love to connect, learn and experience peace and contentment.

~ 8 ~

Cosmic Reality is boundless and formless but yields to countless energies and physical realties. It is through our soul that we can transcend our physical and experiential realties to be at one with the One.

~ 9 ~

From the absolute truth of Oneness emerge countless universes and other relative realties and truth. The original divine Truth remains constant whilst all of creation emerges and subsides.

~ 10 ~

Our world of dualities emanates from the original Unity and returns to It. Knowledges are at numerous levels and at the highest level the knower loses identity into knowledge itself. There is no more 'you' following such an awakening.

~ 11 ~

What we refer to as knowledge mostly reveals cause and effect, as well as relationships in events and situations. The ultimate knowledge is the cosmic Light from which all other knowledges and lights come about.

~ 12 ~

Earthly knowledge is within the limitations of cause and effect and as such is changeable, whereas true knowledge is to do with absolute Unity before dualities.

~ 13 ~

Terrestrial knowledge is due to the celestial soul and is dependent on that timeless constancy.

~ 14 ~

From the cosmic Oneness the mysterious event of creation brought about duality, plurality and multiplicity. Whenever you transcend all of these experiences you reach the origin from which everything has emanated.

~ 15 ~

The present moment is the product and child of the past and the mother of the future. It is only the now that carries the magic of ongoingness and timelessness.

~ 16 ~

The human soul is divine and timeless; it is that which gives rise to the illusion of individual biographies, the shadows of ego and the fantasy of independence.

~ 17 ~

The human composition straddles two zones of consciousness. One is full cosmic consciousness emanating from the soul or spirit and the other is conditioned consciousness, which gives us the illusion of identity, ego and animal tendencies. When a person has awakened to the soul within, the animal self will interfere least with the individual's steadiness and contentment in life.

~ 18 ~

When you awaken to the truth of soul or spirit you understand the relative and temporary reality of the physical and material world. If you have not awakened to that truth then the world within space and time becomes the dominant reality for you with all its limitations and insecurities.

~ 19 ~

If you have fully awakened to the truth of the eternal soul within you, worldly events will not overwhelm you.

~ 20 ~

The soul shines with the light of the Absolute and the ego-self is a shadow that indicates its origin.

~ 21 ~

Conditioned consciousness simply indicates higher levels of consciousness and when you are aware of full consciousness then you don't deny lower consciousness nor does it afflict you.

~ 22 ~

The mind links the absolute with the relative.
One side it is linked to your soul and the other
energizes the lower-self and ego.

~ 23 ~

Consciousness starts with awareness of
various shadows and levels of conditioned
consciousness. Such conditionality often
causes suffering and sorrow until your focus
shows the ultimate consciousness, which is
your own eternal soul.

~ 24 ~

Conditioned consciousness is much affected by physical and other discernable material realties, whereas higher consciousness connects all energies and matters due to the light of the essence upon them all.

~ 25 ~

The light of the soul bestows temporary imaginal value to outer forms which in themselves are inert and merely reflect temporary energies and forms.

~ 26 ~

Whatever exists reflects an aspect of the truth, as does every ego.

~ 27 ~

The ego and animal self are shadows of the soul on earth. They simply indicate their origin without any sustainable reality of their own.

~ 28 ~

The source of the ego-self is the divine
soul beyond the limitations of space and
time. When that zone with its radiating
full consciousness is experienced all other
shadows and minor realities vanish bringing
a joyful relief.

~ 29 ~

All earthy realities and identities are mere
shadows of the permanent light of the Source
from which the inner spirit and soul arises.

~ 30 ~

The real you is a divine spirit that is beyond space and time but the apparent earthly you is its shadow, which merely points to its origin. As such the earthly you leads you to the spiritual reality of who you really are. If you do not follow through with focused enquiry, you remain confused and in earthly darkness.

~ 31 ~

When you awaken to the perpetual reality of your own soul, no other existential reality will entice you or mislead you for long.

~ 32 ~

It is through reflection upon all physical and mental realties and by transcending them all that you touch upon the eternally present Truth behind the entire universe.

~ 33 ~

It is your conditioned consciousness that highlights what you focus upon, such as your ego-self, and it is your higher consciousness that beckons you to reveal the truth of the perpetual soul within.

~ 34 ~

Temporary realities are the cause of all suffering and sorrows. They have all arisen from the original source of the permanent divine Truth, which is the origin of your own soul.

~ 35 ~

It's only through experiencing full consciousness that you reach the conclusion that in truth there is only that cosmic Reality that contains everything known and unknown.

~ 36 ~

The drive to investigate and discover can cause distraction as well as encourage the rise in consciousness towards supreme consciousness and the origin of life.

~ 37 ~

All dualities emerge from cosmic Unity and point towards It. Through diligent striving and honesty you will transcend all distractions and be at One with the original Source of attractions. (Humanity cannot thrive without other human beings, yet it is otherness that veils the effulgent light of Oneness).

~ 38 ~

There is one cosmic Actor that enables each of us to temporarily act as though we are independent. Upon realization of our reliance on the One at all times we are liberated from the illusion of choices and confusions, especially that of separate identity.

~ 39 ~

The soul or spirit is beyond limitation or freedom. It belongs to the zone of the infinite and its shadow-ego is like a confused sleepwalker, until it is awakened to its own source of light and truth within the heart and gives in to that glorious state. This is the purpose of our short journey on earth.

~ 40 ~

The soul is ever constant in providing energy to its shadow, the ego-self, which causes darkness, suffering and the illusion of independence from the magnificent and ever-present soul.

Part Four

Synopsis

The Truth or Reality is the cosmic source and cause of all that is known and unknown and that mysterious essence is within your own soul which resides in your heart.

~ 1 ~

Attachments and desires cast a dark shadow on the heart and hinder the experience of full consciousness which can be enhanced through the friendship and presence of an enlightened being.

~ 2 ~

At first one receives information regarding truth. Then one may experience an epiphany or insight. For such a state to be your norm you need the guidance of a being whom you trust to help steady the spark of the light in your own heart.

~ 3 ~

As humans we need to reduce the agitation and confusion of the ego. However, the light that awakens us has always been there but we have not yet ignited our own candle.

~ 4 ~

Trust and attachment to an enlightened being may help to speed up the purification of your heart and your awakening to the light within it.

~ 5 ~

Human consciousness can gain a quantum leap through the light of an enlightened one.

~ 6 ~

In truth there is only God or the Cosmic Spirit that is the cause of all known and unknown. The reality of every living being is that light which can only be known through the shadow which reflects it and points to it as well as being a veil that conceals it.

~ 7 ~

God is the light of lights, the clarity and qualities of these lights are infinite and their essence lies within the soul of the human being.

~ 8 ~

Within your own heart lies the divine soul from which all lights and shadows emerge, including your ego-self.

~ 9 ~

Your soul and its light are veiled by your imagination of the world and your personal independence. To remove these illusions you need to purify your heart and experience complete silence and stillness on a regular basis.

~ 10 ~

Body and mind are intermediate instruments that connect the cosmic soul residing in you with the visible earthly, material, interactive world.

~ 11 ~

Birth and death are conditioned phenomena held by space and time, their origin and destiny is supreme consciousness.

~ 12 ~

The ego-self has no sustainable reality but its purpose is for you to leave these shadows and catch glimpses of the effulgent soul and its constant perfections.

~ 13 ~

All virtues which we aspire to such as generosity, kindness, sacrifices, patience, etc., help our consciousness to rise towards the perfect soul within.

~ 14 ~

The human journey begins with many needs and dependencies; then through faith, trust and spiritual discipline you will realize that at the beginning, in the middle and at the end there was always power of divine light and guidance.

~ 15 ~

It is ignorance to think that you can attain lasting fulfilment through your actions because in truth the cosmic Actor contains every possible action, as well as inaction.

~ 16 ~

Your soul is cosmic and never affected by any changes in space and time. Your body and mind are manifestations that serve as intermediaries between the boundless consciousness and the earthly limitations.

~ 17 ~

The gift of grace and delight is due to your
own soul. Its earthly reflection (which is your
ego and animal-self) can cause you distraction
and sorrow. This is a double gift from God the
most generous, who bestows earthly glimpses
of perfections and a durable state of bliss in
the hereafter.

~ 18 ~

The metaphorical heart within the soul
sparks life and energy to millions of cells and
hundreds of organs within you. You are a
cosmic being undertaking an earthly journey
through the vehicle of your body and mind.

~ 19 ~

Supreme consciousness gives rise to conditioned, limited and human consciousness. This state requires a rekindling of its connection with origin. This is attained by will and effort; otherwise the illusion of independence and separation elicits much suffering by the conditioned mind.

~ 20 ~

Your soul is cosmic and is inseparable from original cause of the universe. What veils that immense perfection and beauty is the illusion of distance and separation which gives rise to the dark notion of ego, independence and your ability to do whatever you wish.

~ 21 ~

The ultimate challenge for any intelligent human being is to interact and relate to dualities which are the foundation of mental differentiations. The ultimate challenge is to see these dualities as complimentary rather than in opposition to each other. They all emerged from the One and point towards their origin.

~ 22 ~

Your soul resides within your own heart and transmits the cosmic lights and energies that we call life forces. It is only through the prism of your own mind that you experience attraction or repulsion to things, persons or survival drives which can be a hindrance to arrival at the truth of the All-Encompassing Oneness.

~ 23 ~

Your soul is the ultimate mystery and the greatest treasure, if you do not realize that you remain discontent and insecure.

~ 24 ~

Through spiritual discipline, regular meditation, total stillness and silence your consciousness will climb the ladder towards its origin.

~ 25 ~

Our desire for knowledge is a natural drive to attain quality of life without sorrow or misery. The source of all knowledge lies within you and is transmitted from your own soul.

~ 26 ~

The quest for pure consciousness does not deny the experience of numerous other levels of consciousness including what we call normal, sleep or post death consciousness, as everything emanates from the pure essence which is also its destiny.

~ 27 ~

Our so-called normal daily consciousness is a mere shadow of higher consciousness and with reflection we may realize that it merely indicates its origin in every situation.

~ 28 ~

There are two zones that are clearly different in our life experience. One is the conditioned consciousness we share with each other; the other level may be experienced as a flash of reality and is not subject to space, time or change, as it is from that higher quantum realm which we aspire to and where our soul resides.

~ 29 ~

It is through higher intelligence that we go beyond all human struggle and attempts to be awakened to Truth. It is through spiritual intelligence that we come to accept and celebrate the truth that there is only the eternal Truth wherever you look.

~ 30 ~

An enlightened being is in constant connection with full consciousness without denial of lower levels of connectedness. It is just that there are no more fears, sorrow or desires for acquisition or change.

~ 31 ~

When you awaken to higher consciousness the so-called you is fully absorbed in the energy of that consciousness and what remains is only a trace of the so-called you. You are now equally content to remain longer, conditioned by body and mind or to leave them where they belong.

~ 32 ~

In truth our so-called normal waking state is a type of a dream. In fact human life encompasses numerous states of hazy consciousness and imagination which are energized by the consciousness of our own soul.

~ 33 ~

All conduct (action or inaction) has a reaction which balances it. Consequently our intentions and conduct will have a repercussion. It is only when you simply become the pure instrument of the divine light within your own heart that you transcend or circumvent the universal law of action and reaction.

~ 34 ~

It is in human nature to desire what is familiar and seek the ways and means to be at ease and receptive to a wider and deeper goodness. The final stage of that is enlightenment itself - not restricted to any time or place.

~ 35 ~

Knowledge is at numerous levels. In the initial stages there is a natural curiosity for discovery. You will be given the knowledge that is appropriate for your requirements. The final stage is when all visible realities and energies within them are realized to be in a unitive state declaring the cosmic sacred Oneness.

~ 36 ~

Secular learning and training enhances human ability to interact within the limitations of space and time and can bring about material comfort and ease. As for celestial learning and spirituality, the laws are known only by Truth Itself. The entrance to such Truth is by abandoning all notions of knowledge, rationality and understanding that you have been training to acquire. Going to the ocean you take what you consider to be appropriate clothing or gear but if you are an ocean creature you simply dive into it without any encumbrance. Truth is your origin and destiny and now you need to be at home with It.

~ 37 ~

Anything that enhances your ego, gross or subtle, is an additional veil upon the light of your own soul.

~ 38 ~

When you have awakened to your true reality which is the soul within your heart then all aspects to do with your lower animal self lose the importance that you had previously given them.

~ 39 ~

All experiences and events are within the earthly, terrestrial reality, duality and plurality. In order to avoid affliction and suffering, reference to the higher light of your soul before making a choice or action, is necessary. In this temporary existence you can only conduct yourself in a manner that is appropriate for that moment and in that place. Everything constantly changes, except for the light of the Essence.

~ 40 ~

The light of higher consciousness in your own heart is eternal but events and experiences in time are temporally endorsed by the Absolute. Nothing can ever be satisfactory for a continuous duration of time.

List of Recent Publications by Shaykh Fadhlalla Haeri

Universal Quran: Selected Verses for All Times

Quran 50 Vital Verses

Spectrum of Reality: Sufi Insights

The Garden of Meaning

Sufi Encounters: Sharing the Wisdom of the
Enlightened Sufis

For more information on books by Shaykh Fadhlalla
Haeri please visit:

www.zahrapublications.pub

For audiobooks by Shaykh Fadhlalla Haeri visit:

https://www.audible.com/search?
searchNarrator=Shaykh+Fadhlalla-Haeri

For more information on the work of the Shaykh
Fadhllala Haeri Foundation please visit:

www.sfhfoundation.com

To listen and watch talks by Shaykh Fadhlalla Haeri
please visit the SFH Foundation YouTube Channel at:

https://youtube.com/c/SFHFoundation

AUTHOR'S BIOGRAPHY

SHAYKH FADHLALLA HAERI

Sufi, mystic and visionary, Shaykh Fadhlalla Haeri is an enlightened spiritual master. His life and works serve as a reminder that spirituality is a science and an art vitally relevant to our times.

Acknowledged as a master of self-knowledge and a spiritual philosopher, Shaykh Fadhlalla Haeri's role as a teacher grew naturally out of his own quest for self-fulfilment.

His informed awareness of the world around him compelled him to seek a truth that would reconcile the past with the present, the East with the West, the worldly with the spiritual. A link between the ancient wisdom teachings and our present time. He is a descendant of five generations of well-known and revered spiritual leaders, he has taught students throughout the world for over 40 years.

www.ingramcontent.com/pod-product-compliance
Lightning Source LLC
Chambersburg PA
CBHW070621050426
42450CB00011B/3101